Strokes of Color

An Adult Coloring Book for Stroke Survivors

Laura De La Cruz

Foreword by Cynthia Gamez

High Chaparral Publishing
75 County Road A074
Chaparral, NM 88081

A stroke can be debilitating, often leaving patients without the use of one side of their body and wheel chair bound. Anger, denial, and depression set in and it is difficult for caregivers to help stroke victims find meaning in their lives. Often stroke victims must be placed in nursing facilities and receive physical, occupational, and speech therapy. Family members will visit the victim, but are provided with few tools and resources to help structure that visit. It is also difficult for the family member to think of activities that will keep their loved one entertained and distract them from their situation.

With that in mind, when my father had a stroke, I was shocked at how little is available to help structure the family visits. Much of the activity centers around meal time and physical therapy. I started looking for projects that my father could do, like teaching him how to write his name again or reading together. I bought paints and we painted pictures. It was a struggle to keep him from tipping the paint containers, holding up the canvas without all the required artists' tools. So, I thought I would look for a very simple coloring book for him, since coloring books are all the craze right now. But, no luck.

This coloring book was developed by my very dear, long time friend Laura de la Cruz for my father. Although the art is very simple in design, it is perfect for a stroke victim because the lines are clearly defined and the chance of success is better than an open canvas. You will need this book. It is designed so that you can tear out pages and color or you can use these as guides to transfer over to a canvas. If you color on this book, you will want to use markers or crayons. If you transfer this onto a canvas or paper designed for water colors, get some bright acrylic colors. Water color is ideal and I recommend buying inexpensive watercolor paints that are for the beginning artist.
Your loved one will complain and say that he or she is not an artist. A strategy you can use is to say that you are trying to develop the "hand-eye" coordination skills and think of this as art therapy. Find quiet spot, put some soothing music on, and spend an hour painting or coloring. This will help both of you relax and enjoy your time together.

Cynthia Gamez

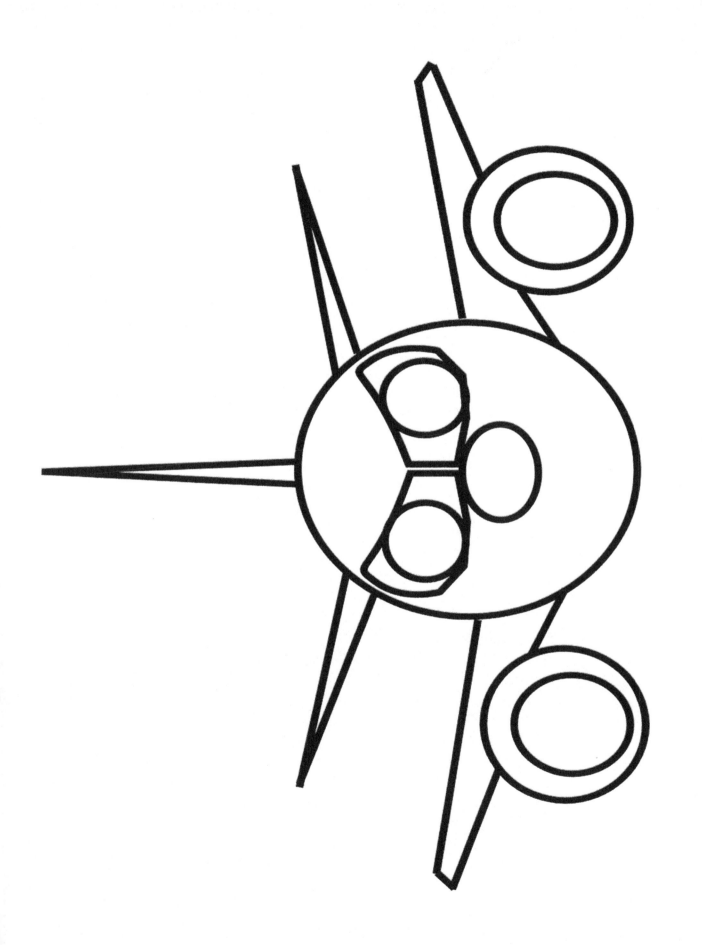

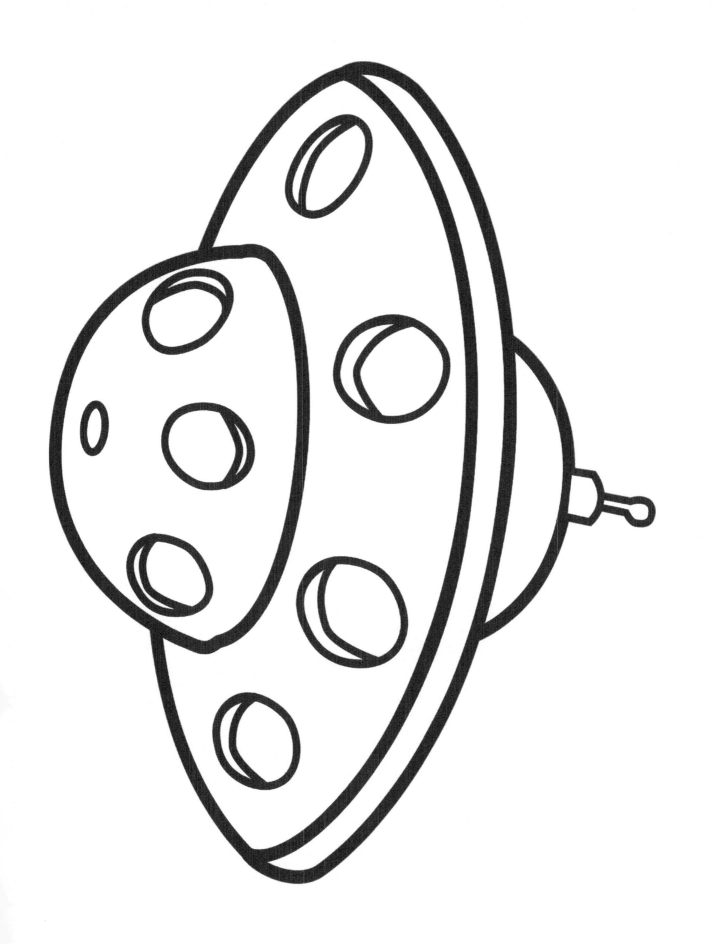

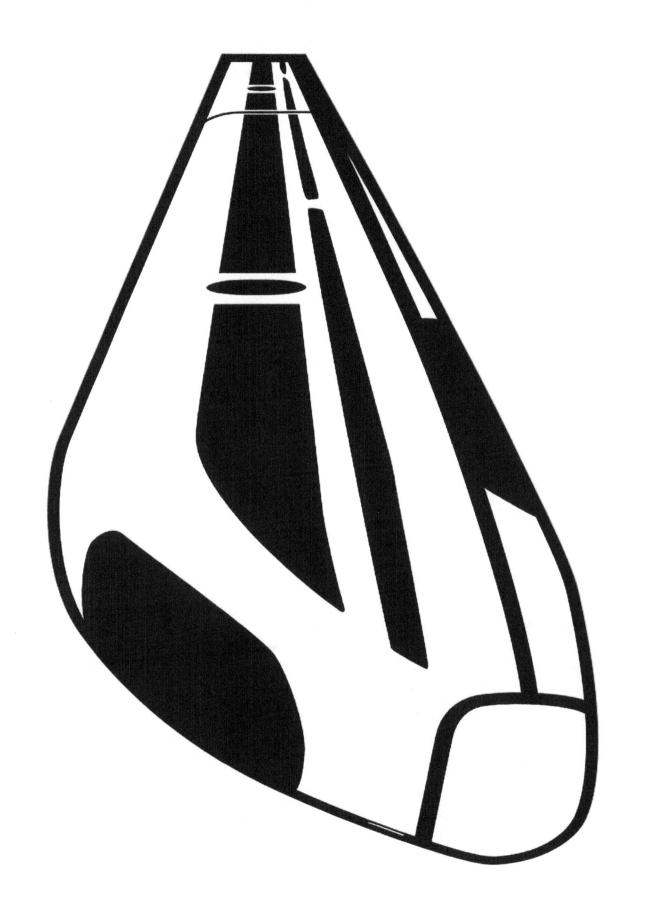

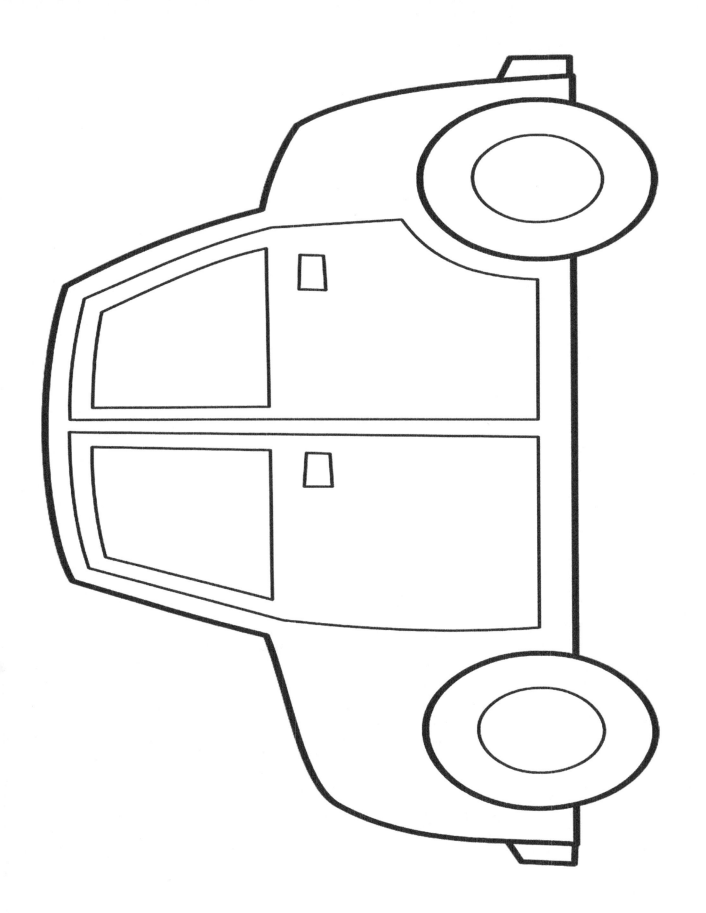

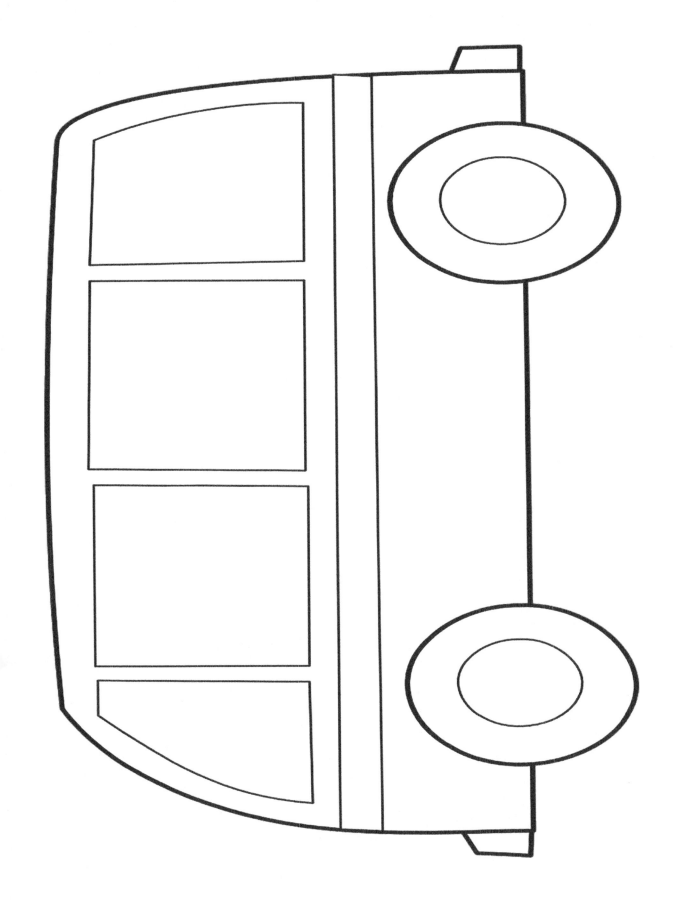

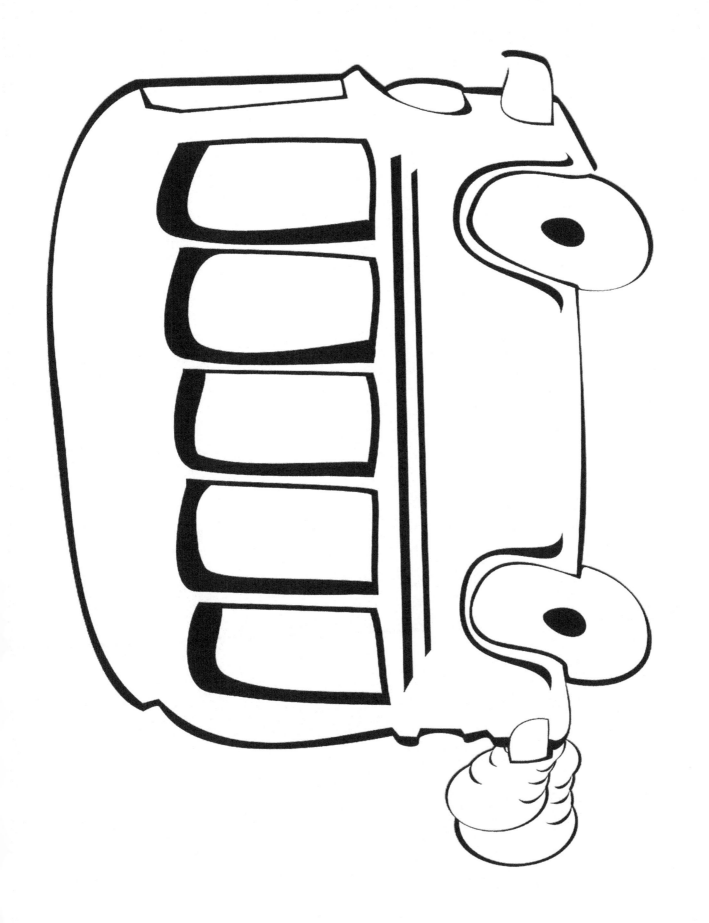

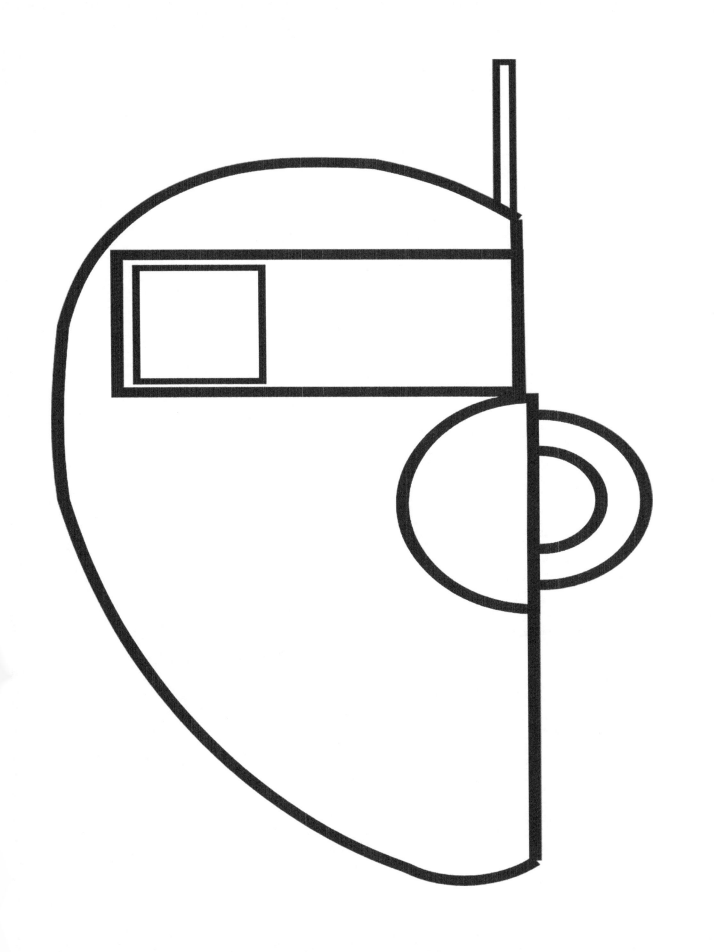

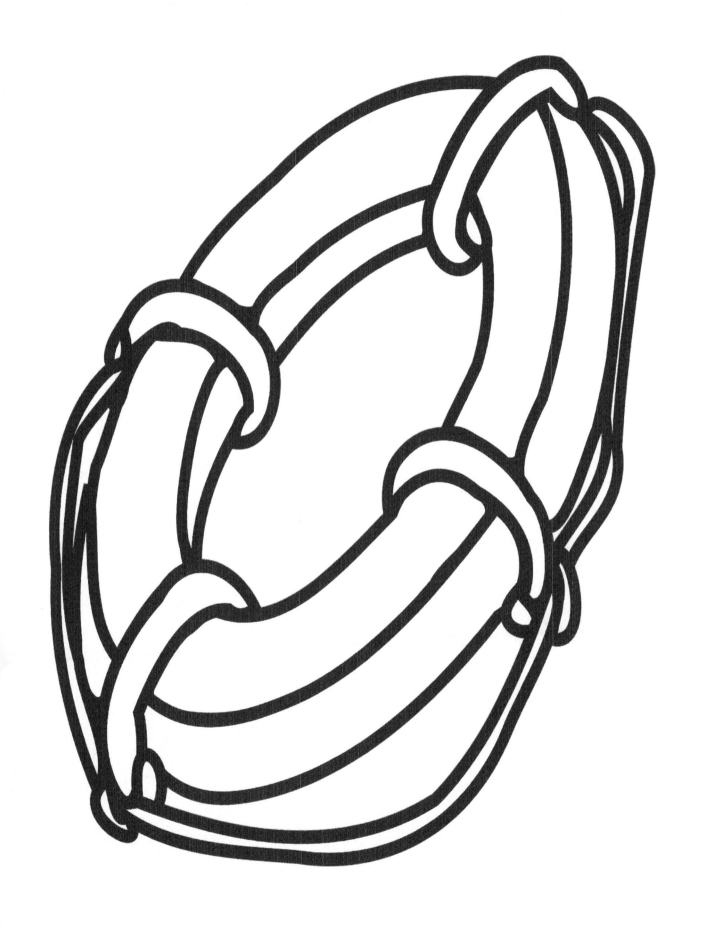

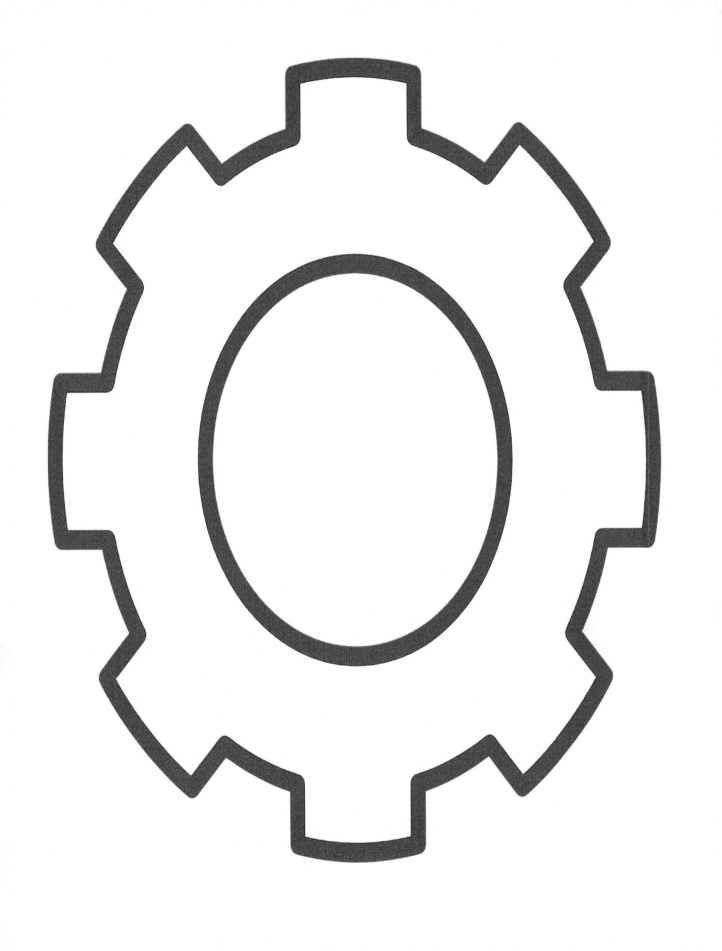

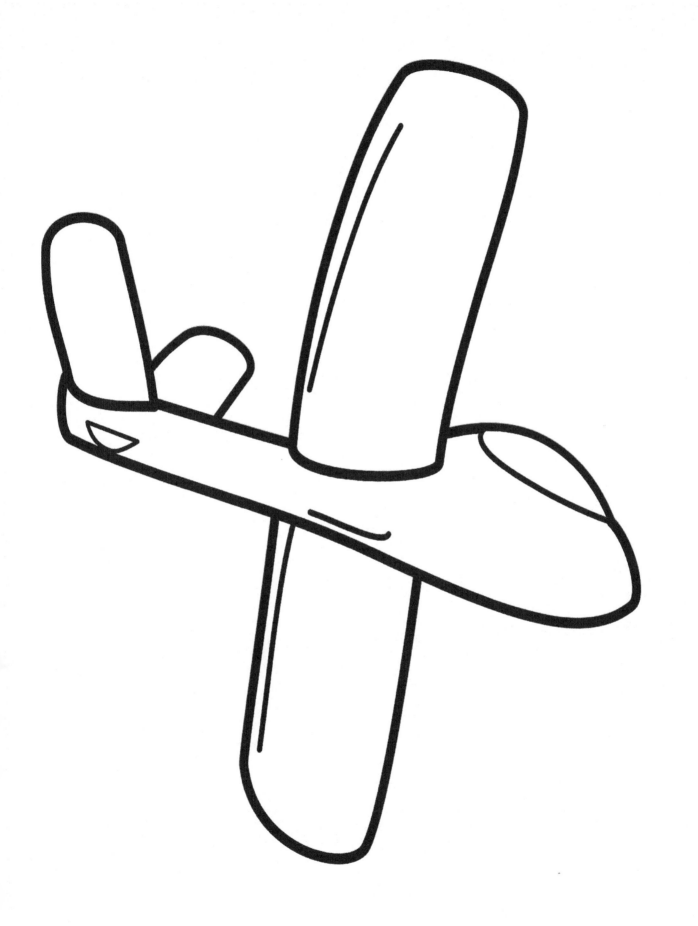

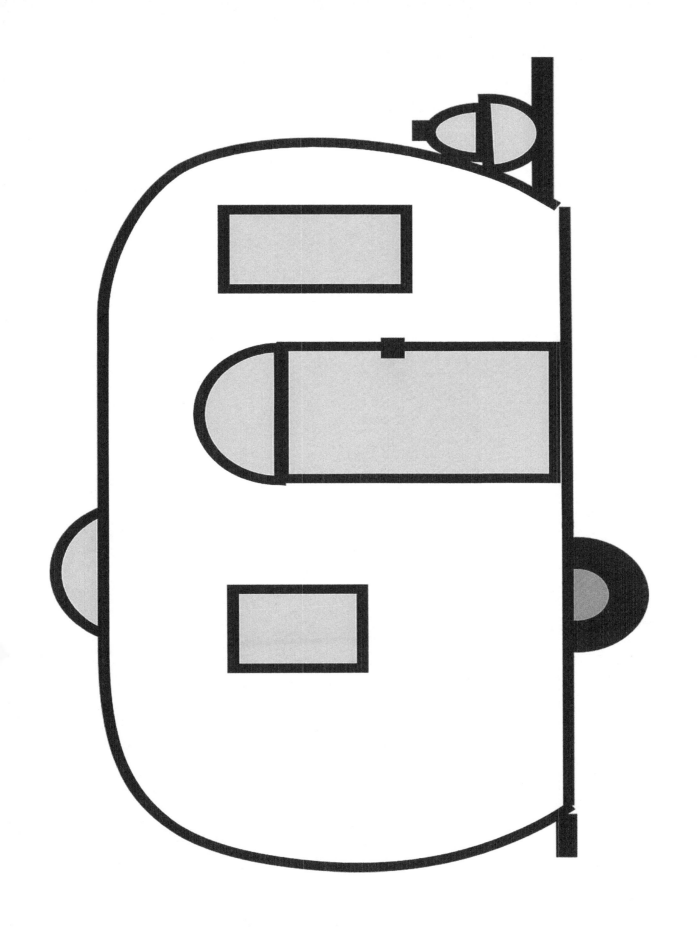

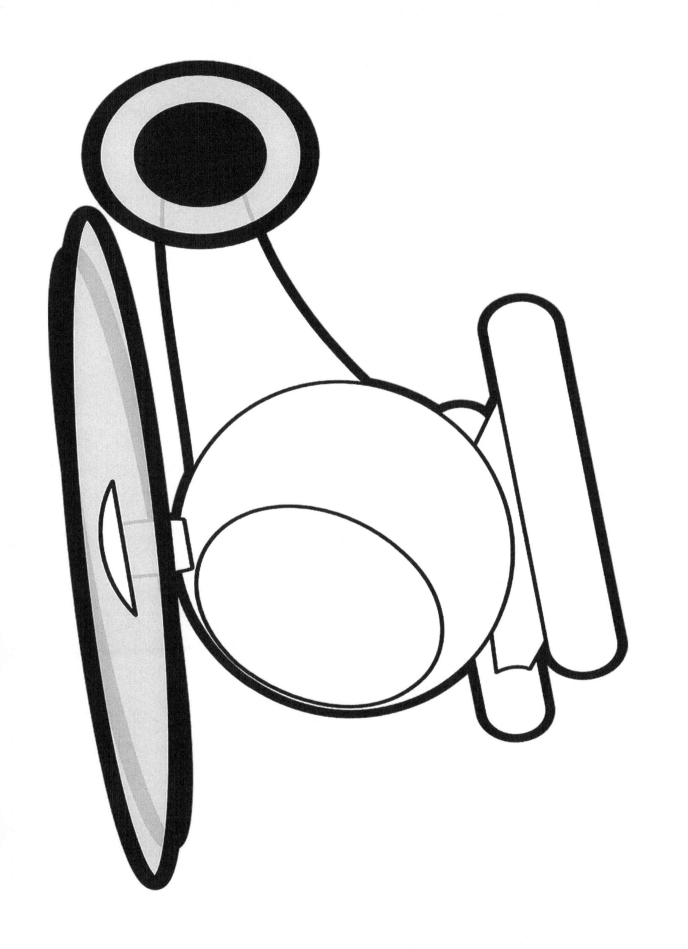

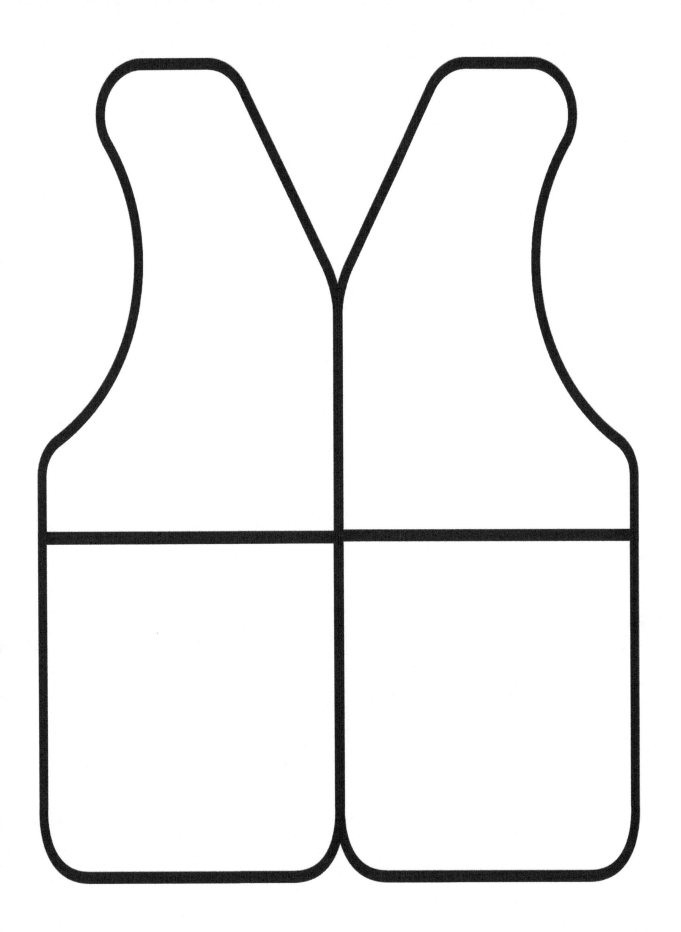

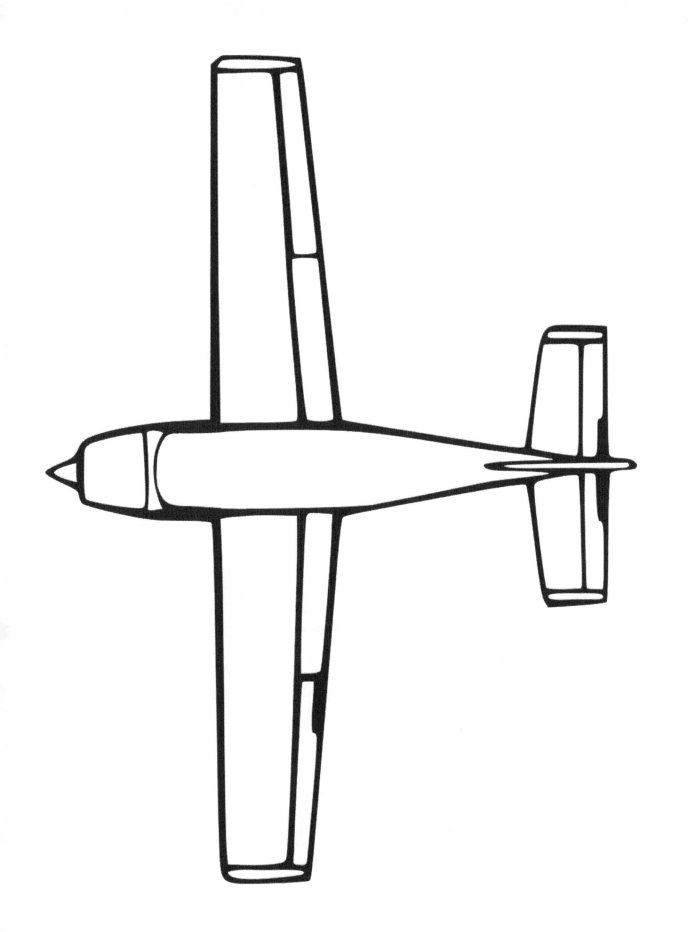

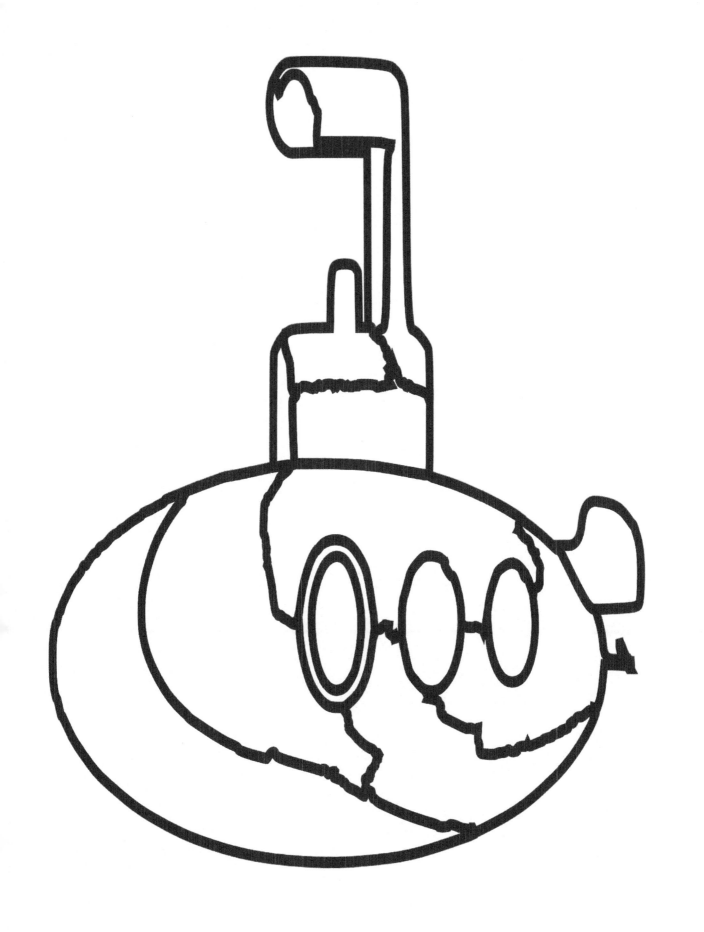

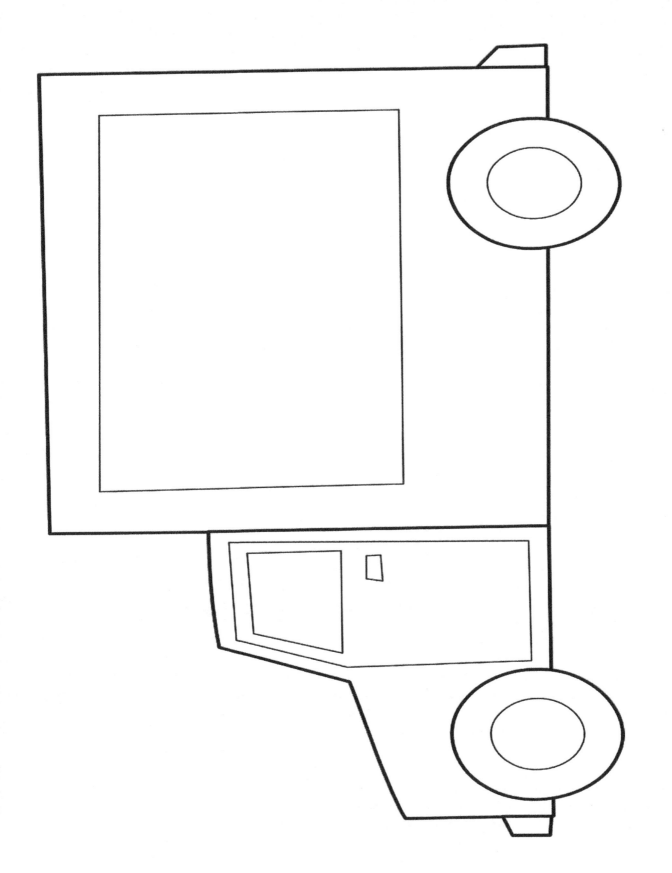

Thank you for purchasing this book. If you found it useful for your loved one, please leave a positive review.

Your family is in our thoughts and prayers.

Laura & Cynthia